Disclai

MW00932629

This publication is intended .. p. ....
authoritative information in regard to the subject matter
covered. It is distributed with the understanding that the
publisher, author, and all contributors are not engaged in
rendering legal, accounting, or other professional
services. If legal, tax, or other expert assistance is
required, the services of a competent professional
should be sought.

This book is intended for instructional purposes
only. Every effort has been made to reflect the applicable
laws as of the date of the publication of this book.
However, this is a dynamic field of endeavor in which new
laws are enacted, old laws revised and/or reinterpreted
on a continuing basis, and where statutes, rulings and
precedential case law are constantly changing. Readers
are advised to proceed with the techniques described
herein with due caution.

Neither the author, printers, licensees, nor
distributors make any warranties, expressed or implied,
about the merchantability or fitness for any particular use
of this product.

Reproduction or translation of any part of this
work without permission of the copyright owner is
unlawful and strictly prohibited.

5701 W. Slaughter Ln. A 130-132
Austin, TX 78749
TaxSaleArbitrage.com
Support@TaxSaleArbitrage.com

WELCOME to MY World

I 've been investing in real estate for the past seventeen years and many people know me as the "Probate Goldmine Real Estate Guy." During the course of hundreds of deals, I ran into a little loophole that was costing normal citizens their homes, monies owed to them AND that money was being pocketed by the government.

A few months of research and reverse engineering created a fool-proof system for being able to requisition these monies on behalf of anyone whom is owed. The best part of being able to help those people claim their money is that you can earn a finder's fee.

Anyone with a phone and a computer can do this business. No driving required, no land-lording headaches, no brick and mortar overhead expenses, no employees, no pulling comps, no bidding wars. It is one of the simplest entrepreneurial opportunities I've ever stumbled upon.

With this book, you are granted a 7-day free trial of REISecrets Society. You received the registration link via email so please check your spam folder. In the VIP membership site, which you will have access to once you become a full VIP member in 7 days, you will find a course called Quick Cash Conversions. It is the course we designed specifically for people who are intrigued by this money making option and are interested in more training. It is available for members ONLY so do not cancel your membership.

On top of the tremendous benefits of being a member, which include: interviews with hundreds of professionals in MY sphere of influence whom are entrepreneurs across all business models, student testimonials, interviews with students who are CRUSHING it, free copies of my unlaunched courses AND the opportunity to jump on a call with me once a week so I can help you with ANYTHING you are interested in.

I'd like to thank my beautiful wife, Hilary for being the most amazing woman I've ever known. She has enriched my life in ways I knew not possible. Her gifts as a mother never go unnoticed as she ushers our three children into the formative years.

For more information check out www.taxsalearbitrage.com

Best,

Stacy Kellams

Section One
Unclaimed Money

What are Unclaimed Funds?

Generally, unclaimed funds are any money held by any institution or government agency that belongs to an individual or entity that has not claimed it.

Some examples are unpaid insurance proceeds, stock dividends, retirement benefits, inheritance proceeds, income tax refunds, property tax refunds, oil and gas royalties, artist royalties, and uncollected wages…

The list goes on …

Our focus is specific to the unclaimed excess funds created from tax sales. Did you know that within 24 months of being behind of property taxes, the government can seize your property and sell it to satisfy those overdue taxes?

Can you imagine being told you have to move out of your home, pack up your children and vacate the only home they have ever known? Let's say your house it paid for, but your life circumstances have changed due to loss of a job, death of a family member, bankruptcy or illness. Your house needs too much work to put on the market so you are between a rock and a hard place.

Suddenly, the government seizes the property and sells it at auction.

Here is some math:

Fair market value for the house: $54,000.00

Over due taxes: $10,000.00

Sale price at auction: $34,000.00

After the government pays that tax debt- there will be $24,000.00 left over. When property is sold at tax foreclosure sale and is sold for more than what is owed on the property, excess funds, sometimes called overbids, overages, excess proceeds or surplus funds, are created.

The owner at the time of the sale (the one losing the property) is generally supposed to receive those excess funds. However, they rarely receive the money.

The person often moves without a forwarding address so the one required notice of overage is sent to the last known address ... the address of the property taken out from under them.

There is no incentive for the government to find them. In fact, if the person does not claim the money within a certain time, the government gets to keep it.

The person owed the money (called the "claimant") often doesn't realize they are owed money at all. We locate the claimants and help them to recover their money before this happens.

After we find the claimant and notify them of their claim, our goal is to sign an agreement to process their claim for them for 10 to 40% or more of the amount of the claim. We do all the work and get paid when the claim is paid so there is no risk for the claimant as they are receiving money they did not know about.

After we receive a check from the agency, we disburse the claimant their funds after deducting expenses and our fee.

Do Excess Funds Exist in your Area?

Maybe. You have to know the law in your area.

Research Questions:

- What legal issues exist in that area?
- Does that area allow excess funds to be paid to the prior owner?
- What are the limits on what money locators can charge?
- Are there any license requirements for money locators?
- Do these money locator laws apply to agency foreclosure excess funds or just to state level unclaimed funds?

Many states have "money finder laws" or "locator laws" that limit the amount you can receive for finding the claimant and processing the claim. For example, Florida requires that money locators are either private detectives, CPAs, or attorneys registered with the state and can only receive 20% and a maximum of $1,000 per account unless you meet additional requirements.

In addition, not all states let the claimant keep the excess funds. In those states, the law is written so that the excess funds go directly to the government. Check our Best States Guide to make sure the state you are looking at has tax sale excess funds (sometimes called overbids, overages, surplus funds, excess proceeds).

Why It Doesn't Matter?

What if the state you live in doesn't have excess funds available or is not in the list of best states? It doesn't matter what state you work deals in. I have many students who live in the UK and Canada who have great success processing claims here in the US. That is precisely why this is the ultimate "virtual" business.

You can do it from anywhere.

What you need to Get Started

Access to a phone and a computer. I have one student who uses the computer at her "local" library. She drives every morning twenty minutes, works a few hours and drives home.

I'm going to show you how to get the list of claimants. How to locate the claimant on the list. How to contact the claimant and get the necessary documents signed. How to file the claim and get paid.

All you need to do right now is decide on a goal. What is it that you want? More money? More time with your family? A business you can do in your underwear and get out of grid-lock traffic? What is your motivating factor?

Then I want you to engage the mindset that you can do anything and will do anything to reach your goals! I can teach you the system but I can't force you to do it. Your goal and mindset are the extra ingredients you need to be successful.

Action Items:

1. **Write down your goals.**

2. **Write down why you want to reach your goals; what will reaching your goals provide you with?**

3. **Research your area laws to find out if excess funds are available, what are the laws, the process, and locator fee limits.**

4. **Decide on an area you want to work.**

Section Two

How do You Know Who is Owed Money?

Each government agency keeps records of these people. Most often it is in the form of a list or spreadsheet. While this information is public record, they may not give it up by mail or email. I've run into a couple who insist you come in in person.

The list is a collection of information on individuals who are owed money due to excess funds remaining after a tax sale.

Ideally, it is a spreadsheet containing the claimant's name, address of the property, tax parcel number, the amount of the overage, the date of sale, and a legal description. However, every list is different and in some agencies, it may not even be a "list." It may be individual claims, not in spreadsheet format, and may only contain some of the claimant information listed above.

Once you decide what area of the country you want to work in, you can begin researching these overages, lists and or excess funds using free search engines.

When you get the right office:

1. Get a name, phone number, and email address of the person responsible for the list.

2. Ask if they require a written public records request or will a verbal one suffice;

3. Ask if there are any fees associated with obtaining the list. Some agencies charge a fee to get the list but it is worth it when you consider making thousands of dollars and only paying $50 or less to get the list. The return on investment is huge!

4. Ask what documents are required to file a claim such as driver's license, copy of social security card, etc. and any specific language that might be required on the claim form, do they require a power of attorney if you are filing a claim for someone else and do they require specific language for the power of attorney, get a copy of the exact language if they do;

5. Ask for a sample claim form.

Always follow-up with emails and calls if you don't receive anything within a reasonable time. And be sure to follow up with a Thank You email when you receive the list.

Every once in a while you will get a agency that is a stickler for the proper public access law reference in order to give you access to their list, so you need to know the public access law pertaining to the agency in which you are working.

Does the request need to be in writing? How long do they have to respond and how are they required to respond? Is there a special public access officer? Are there any fees? If the format exists electronically, do they have to provide it to you that way? Will the agency mail or email the list to you? Check the Public Records Access Guide for more information.

Helpful Tips:

1. Research the law regarding the Public Records Act in the area you are working in. Note: Public Records Act is not the same as the federal Freedom of Information Act – that doesn't apply, its federal law not state law, although some states call their acts Freedom of Information as well).

2. Always remain friendly and professional with everyone you speak to. Never demand or get belligerent with the people on the phone.

3. Don't give up until you get to the person who controls the list.

4. If you simply can't get the list, stop wasting time and move on to another office.

List building is our foundation. We cannot run this business without them. Learn how to get them and you will be on your way to success.

Organizing the Lists

Before you get too far into this business, let me stress how important it is to stay organized. You are going to have multiple lists coming in and multiple deals going all the time in various stages of the process.

It is imperative that you stay organized and have all your information in one central location.

You also need to have your information accessible from anywhere and definitely not on scraps of paper every where. You don't want to be out running an errand and get that call back from a claimant and have no access to their file. Y don't want to write something down on a post-it and loose it.

I highly recommend an online data management system like HighriseHQ.com. You can keep all your deal information in one location, accessible from anywhere that you, or your assistant, have internet.

Go to Highrise http://basecamphq.com/?referrer=STACYKELLAMS to check out their data management system and sign up.

Another system I use is www.teamwork.com

Check both out and see which you prefer.

HighriseHQ.com has a system built to handle leads and files and individual "deals" where teamwork is more of a project management system.

Credibility

There are two separate camps on how to approach a claimant. One would be as a person who has run into this before and has started helping people to recover their funds ... keep in mind, the claimants have been worked over and ripped off by the government.

They have literally lost EVERYTHING and now a business with a scary name is calling them. OR, they are nervous and if you have a business name, a PO box, and a website detailing what you do and why they feel better.

I find it's a personal decision. If you want to go the "business route," you might want to consider the below options.

Here are the top things you need for your credibility proof:

- Website with Your Business Name & Logo

- Business Cards and Letterheads with your Business Name and Logo

- Use e-mail address through your domain name not a gmail, hotmail or yahoo account

- Join the Better Business Bureau (often have to be in business for a certain time before can join.)

- See if need Business License in your state; if so, get it

- Look professional

- As soon as you get a deal done, get a testimonial from the claimant and use that on your site – people want to hear about other people you have helped

Business Entities

There are several ways you can set up your business. Everything from a sole proprietor (single person doing business under your own name) to several different legal entities: C Corporation, S Corporation, Limited Partnership, or Limited Liability Company.

Although you don't have to create an entity to run your business, there are a lot of legal and business reasons you may want to. Asset protection is one of the largest legal reasons for setting up an entity, and I recommend you speak to a legal professional in your area for more advice on which entity is best for you.

From the business standpoint, I personally think your business looks more professional if it is an actual business entity instead of Joe Smith, sole proprietor.

Either way you go, I recommend that you also file a DBA (Doing Business As) in your agency for the company name you choose for your letterheads and website.

I would hold off on spending a ton of money until you start making money.

Mailing Address

Another important consideration is your mailing address. Technology has allowed us to be able to work from anywhere, including home. However, a lot of people working from home don't want their physical home address as their business mailing address.

There are several businesses offering "Virtual Office Plans" now where for a monthly fee, they provide receptionist / message service, physical and mailing address, and you can use office or conference space as needed.

Another less expensive option is mailing services that rent mail boxes with physical addresses, like Mail Boxes, etc. or UPS Store. I recommend using one of these with a Suite address instead of using a P.O. Box.

Important Tips:

While a catchy name for your excess funds business website and letterhead may be great for potential claimants to view, it is sometimes a hindrance when trying to obtain the list from the agency. Some individuals you talk to at the agency don't fully understand how beneficial our services are and may be biased against you just from your contact information when obtaining the list.

When obtaining lists and dealing with the agency, we generally use our official entity name and then use our DBA (doing business as) name on our website and dealing with claimants.

I recommend using different email accounts and letterheads for dealing with agencies vs. dealing with claimants. I suggest setting up your business entity and that is what you use to contact agencies, set up bank accounts, etc. Then do DBA for your unclaimed funds site with the business name you use for marketing to claimants.

Action Items:

1. **Set up online data / contact management system like Highrise.**

2. **Find out what business licenses are required.**

3. **Decide on business name, file necessary business paperwork with city and state.**

4. **Set up bank account.**

5. **Get a website for your business.**

6. **Create letterheads.**

Section Three
Finding the Claimant Research

Using Free Sites

After we get the list and decide which claims we are going to focus on, we start looking for the person named on the list. There are many free online services you can try such as www.whitepages.com , www.people.yahoo.com, or just by doing a Google search for the person.

And don't forget to check the social network sites such as www.facebook.com, www.classmates.com , or www.linkedin.com.

Using social media is another effective tool to track down claimants or relatives of claimants. Facebook for example has over 500 million users worldwide. It's free to setup an account if you don't already have one. Searching for a claimant is pretty simple. You can type in the claimant's name and search by city or state. Then simply send them a message explaining what you are trying to accomplish.

Here are some sample Messages you can try:

Sample One: " Hi Jane, I've been trying to find you. I found a valuable item that I think belongs to you. Please contact me as soon as possible so I can make sure I have the right person. Thanks, Stacy"

Sample Two: " Hi Bob, I located some unclaimed funds that I think may belong to you. Please contact me so that I can make sure I have the right person and tell you what I found. I would not want to see you lose money that is owed to you so please contact me. Thanks, Stacy"

I recommend keeping your standard messages in your contact management system so that you can copy and paste it into the message instead of drafting it from scratch every time. This will save you some time and you also want to test and track your messages to see which get the best responses.

Facebook also allows you to setup a business fanpage for your Excess Funds business. This is another way to give your business some extra online credibility and free advertising.

Another site to use is www.Obituaries.com . They have a small fee to do searches on their website. If you know that a claimant is deceased and you're having trouble finding the heirs through the probate court, this is another way to track them down.

If you don't have any luck finding the person with a quick search using one of those methods, there are several sites that you can pay to be a member and get a more extensive search for the person you are looking for.

Paid Sites

First off for those of you who may not be familiar with Accurint, Intelius, and Merlin Data let me explain what these systems are and why these tools are a MUST in the Excess Funds business.

These are both what are called "skip tracing" tools. What is skip tracing? Skip tracing is a process that allows you to search for a specific person by name in order to obtain contact information about them. Contact information such as phone numbers, current and prior addresses, and even court documents in some cases.

In the old days, you had to flip through phone books to find someone. These days, with all of the technological advances we can use tools like these on the computer to track down anyone in the world.

I want to take a minute to guide you through and briefly tell you how you can set these systems up for your business. I will also show you the different types of reports you can run, and what information is important when pulling your reports to find a claimant.

Setup of these services is quite simple. The sites mentioned above can be setup at their websites listed here:

www.Accurint.com

www.Intelius.com , go to our easy affiliate link at http://www.kqzyfj.com/click-3765911-10794544

www.MerlinData.com

www.tlo.com

Accurint:

This is probably the best out of the 3 in my opinion. It is also more expensive and has a much more in depth pre-screening process when setting it up. These tools can be abused in the wrong hands so to prevent that from happening, Accurint wants to ensure you will not abuse the power when using their services. You can get your account setup by visiting their website at www.Accurint.com or by calling *1.888.332.8244. Option 2.*

Intelius:

We frequently use Intelius in our business and the results have been good. If for some reason you cannot afford or qualify for Accurint, this is a great alternative. It is easier to get setup and it is also less expensive. In addition, you get your own personal account representative that you can call anytime to help answer questions. The best program to use is the pre-paid "credits" option. Basically for a flat fee upfront payment, Intelius will give you 500 credits.

For example, you pay let's say $130 up front and receive 500 report credits. Each time you run a report for a claimant that is only 1 credit. As you can see this is pretty cheap. To check their current prices and other information visit http://www.kqzyfj.com/click-3765911-10794544 .

Merlin Data:

Merlin is a great site to use as well. They have many different programs to suit your needs for this business. They have a full price sheet breakdown they can email you to make your choices easier. We have not used this one as much as the others, but we know other people who really like it.

Types of Reports

Each site has different names for the types of reports you can run. It can get quite overwhelming with the assortment of choices.

You can get everything from the very basic report to in depth court records, aviation registration info, bankruptcy reports, criminal records, liens & judgments, and a long list of other reports.

Fortunately, when searching for claimant's you only need one of these reports to track them down in most case and it's one of the least expensive reports offered.

We pulled every single report there is when we first started in this business. So I can tell you which reports work and all of the ones that you do not need. Let's stick to mentioning the reports that you do need.

With Accurint, 99% of the time you will be pulling the "Finder Report." This report will give you all of the information you will need at the most reasonable cost. As of this writing it is just a couple bucks per report.

With Intellius the report you will need to run is called "People Search" report. This allows you to type in a claimant's name and search by State. This report will give links to relatives as well so you can call them in order to get in touch with the claimant.

What do you look for in your reports?

The skip tracing companies keep their information very organized in these reports. Typically what you will see in an Accurint report for example is all of the most important contact information on the top of the report. Information such as the claimant's current known phone number and address. It goes down from there listing previous addresses, neighbors, 1st degree relatives, 2nd degree relatives, and 3rd degree relatives.

It also has a "known associates" listing which can be the claimant's friends. Most of the time by calling all the numbers on this report you can track the claimant down. It is just a numbers game. The more phone calls you make the better your chances of contacting the claimant and making a deal.

It is best to make your calls in the following order:

1st – To the actual claimant's current phone number

2nd – All 1st, 2nd, 3rd degree relatives

3rd – Known Associates

4th – Neighbors.

5th – Any others including previous employers.

Don't give up calling numbers on the report until you either reach the claimant or can get a physical address and/or email address for someone who knows or may know where the claimant is located.

These reports will often tell you if the claimant has died. This is very important to note, because you will have to shift gears and track down the heirs of the claimant at that point. Luckily this can often times be easier than finding a claimant that is living believe it or not. 90% of the probate courts in the U.S. will require either a case number or name of a deceased person in order to gain access to a probate file. This makes it much easier for you having the claimant's name on hand. Everything you will need to know is in that probate file usually.

Important Tip:

Also be sure to make a note in your deal file if the report shows that the claimant has the same address as the property that was sold. We had a case where the winning bidder at the tax foreclosure sale allowed the prior owner to remain in the home. When we contacted the claimant, he did not know he had excess funds and we discovered that he wanted to exercise his right of redemption to keep the property.

Action Items:

1. **Review various skip tracing sites and try one.**

2. **Pull a report on yourself or your first claimant**

3. **Review the report**

NOTES

Section Four

Contacting the Claimant

The list is key but contacting claimants equals cash! Don't spend all your time getting lists. If you're not contacting claimants you're not getting deals done. No deal means no cash and that's not what we want.

Once you have at least one list, start contacting claimants. If you can't find a good phone number or address for the claimant start calling and sending letters to the claimant's relatives. Don't give up until you have exhausted the list of names in your skip tracing report.

I recommend using the free online sources first. Facebook, linkedin and Google, Yahoo and BING have made finding people quick, easy and free. When I first started doing this, information was much more difficult to come by and much more expensive.

Don't get me wrong, once you make some money, close a few deals and really ramp things up, using a private detective or a background checking service might be very wise for larger claims.

Managing Your List

You will find there are a lot of claimants and you need to decide which ones to pursue and which ones to cut from your list. You want to pick the best ones and start running your reports to track down the claimant.

Picking the Best:

First, cut the claims expiring in less than 1 month. It is going to take some time to find your claimant, deal with the agency and get all the paperwork signed and filed. I suggest giving yourself at least 3 months from the claim expiration date when you first get started.

Second, decide what your dollar limit is, the least dollar claim amount you are willing to pursue. Is your limit $2,000, $5,000, more or less? Remove all the claims that are below your dollar limit.

Third, remove all the ones that are too complicated. Your criteria for this may change a little as you get more experience but don't try to go after a deal where the claimant died and left 6 heirs and no one knows where 2 of them are for your first deal. There are a lot of easy deals out there so don't waste your time on the hard ones when you are still learning the business.

As a general rule, the further the claimant lives from the Agency where the excess funds are located the better for us. It's much harder for the claimant to just walk down there and pick the money after we have done all the work.

Beginners:

I highly recommend that beginners make at least 50 to 100 calls on lower end claims, claims under $5,000, until they are confident on the phone. Reasons to focus on claims under $5,000:

1. Great for beginners who are terrified to call claimants and need practice talking to claimants. Don't practice on the high dollar claims. Get your practice in on the claims that you won't be disappointed about losing.
2. Less competition. Most people in the unclaimed funds business go from the top down, starting with the highest claims and working down. If you specialize in low claims and can get good at doing them fast in high volume you'll have very little competition.
3. Claimants are often more willing to assign funds over. Lower dollar amount = claimant not caring as much since it isn't a whole lot of cash.

With small claims you need to give yourself a time limit. Decide how much time you will spend trying to find a claimant and make a deal. Once that limit is reached, it may become counterproductive and unprofitable continuing to pursue a dead lead.

A Note about Claims Expiring in Less than ONE MONTH:

If you run into this scenario..... Obviously time is of CRITICAL importance. I would do two things immediately... call the agency and:

(1)   find out the turnaround time between document submittal to check issuance from that agency. If they say 3 weeks or less, that's great news.

(2)   make SURE the money is still there in the Treasurer's account.

Good news about short time frame claims:

1. Gives the claimant a HUGE sense of urgency to do whatever it takes to get it done FAST.

2. Many Agencies will "stop the clock" for you. In other words. Even though the claims can legally escheat within the 30 days. Many Agencies will let you submit the documents and if that claim takes 2 months to close you are safe because you got all documents submitted BEFORE the clock runs out on the escheat date. Make sure you ask them this upfront to see if they will do it. Do not assume they will!

The Yes, No's and Maybe's

You called the claimant and got them to agree to work with you. Great job! Pat yourself on the back because like any business it's a numbers game. Not everyone you call will sign up and some may not even believe you. So take a second to pat yourself on the back when you get the "Yes". Then get busy sending your notary to get everything signed as soon as possible and preferably within the 24 to 48 hours after your call with the claimant.

The "No" is a little tougher to take but at least you can mark them off the list and narrow your list to only the good ones. We will sometimes do a follow-up post-card or letter mailing to the claimant so that our name and contact info is in front of them in case the change their mind. Our follow-up direct mail may even offer to buy their right to claim since they are not interested. Offering them a few hundred dollars just to pay their right to claim will sometimes make them curious and call you back or sometimes will result in an Assignment of Right. Be sure the agency you are working in is familiar with assignments before making that deal. You don't want to pay someone and then find out the agency is going to make it impossible to collect.

The "Maybe" answer, definitely not the "yes" you were hoping for but now is your change to follow-up with direct mail and get them hooked. Always put your "maybe's" in your direct mail list and start sending those out the same day you talk to the claimant so that they receive it while they still remember your call.

Frequently Asked Questions:

How did you find this money?

We do extensive research and audit the files of many government agencies and public corporations looking for unclaimed funds and assets owed to people just like you.

How did you find me?

We use many methods to locate people, including web searches, phone calls, and our specialty software. It sometimes takes us several months of researching to locate the right person.

How big is my claim? Where are the funds being held?

We are currently helping lots of other people just like you; however, we are unable to help until we have authorization from you to do further research and prepare all the necessary paperwork to submit your claim.

If you have not already received our agreement from us, please contact us immediately to receive this important document that allows us to do all the work to get your funds to you. Once you have signed our contract for services and the limited power of attorney, we will immediately continue with all the necessary steps to prepare the documents and to submit the claim, and will then be able to give you an exact dollar amount of the claim.

Where did this money come from?

Once you have signed the necessary initial documents,

we can provide you with all the information regarding the claim that we are assisting you with.

When should we start, and how much time do I have to collect my money?

Today! By law, you only have a limited amount of time to claim these funds before the agency is legally allowed to keep your funds for itself. If you miss the deadline for filing the proper paperwork, you will lose your chance at these funds. Don't let that happen. Act now before it's too late!

When will I receive my money?

It usually takes about two weeks after we prepare and file the paperwork for the agency to process the claim. Once it has been approved, we hold the claims check for thirty days to make certain there are no problems with the agency, then we over-night your check straight to you.

Is this legal?

Absolutely it is! If you are the true owner of some unclaimed funds then you have every right to claim them before they are lost to the government. It is also completely legal for us to act as your agent and deal with these agencies on your behalf so that you may use our time and expertise to make sure your claim is filed properly and on time.

Why can't I just find this money myself?

You can, but there is a good chance that you will be unsuccessful, especially since the agencies don't contact you and we had to do extensive research just to get to this point. There is also a lot of correspondence and paperwork involved that must be submitted before the deadline.

We maintain a comprehensive database of sources of funds. It takes weeks and months of searching and knowing where to look and who to communicate with. We also have a staff that deals directly with each agency, prepares all documents necessary, consults with our in-house legal counsel if there are any issues with your claim, and files all the necessary paperwork as needed within the deadline. This is our specialty and we're good at it.

Why should I use your company?

Most of the assets we locate aren't found using the internet, and it's unlikely that you will ever be notified of their existence. The agency holding your funds may ultimately keep them if you don't claim them very soon. How much effort do you really think they put into contacting the rightful owners? They are the ones who benefit if a claim is NOT made.

We've already put in the long hours, hard work and deep digging for you. All you need to do is agree to our proposal and collect the 'Lions share' of the proceeds!

What will it cost me?

Nothing. You will never incur one penny of expense with *Your Company Name*. We pay for everything; notaries, couriers, filing fees, document preparation, everything! We only get paid when your claim gets paid.

Do I have to sign your documents?

Yes. It's the only way we can legally represent you, otherwise the agency will refuse to deal with us. Our contract for services is very simple - there is no confusing language, just a simple agreement about how we split the claim, if successful. We are paid on a contingency basis, which means that we don't get paid unless the money is recovered. All documents that you need to sign pertain only to your particular claim and give us no power relating to anything else in your life. We will not have access to your personal financial information, or the ability to make decisions on your behalf relating to anything other than this claim. All document signings will be done in the presence of a licensed notary public.

I'm just not comfortable with this...what can I do?

There are several things you can and should do right now. Keep in mind there is only a short window of time for you to collect these funds. Talk to your family members or an attorney about it and feel free to have them contact us as well. Our contract for services is available for you to review before hand, just ask one of our specialists.

Can someone else handle this for me?

Absolutely. You can have a family member or trusted advisor call us and we will explain everything to them. You will, however, need to be present for the signing of the documents. We do need the actual claimant's signature and to verify that person's identity (driver's license or other identification) before we can process your claim.

What number should I call?

Toll Free: 888.YourNumber

Email: info@yourBizEmail.com

Section Five

Document Preparation and Signing

You got the list, contacted the claimant, and now you're ready to get the deal going. The first thing you must do, if you haven't already, is find out exactly what the agency needs. Every government office is different and requires different things when filing a claim.

Some agencies will often have their own claim form you must use. Email or call your contact person and ask exactly what documents they will need to file the claim, i.e. their claim form, copy of driver's license, and any other documents they need. Some will want a copy of the Agency Tax Record.

Some agencies will also want a copy of the claimant's social security card. In one of our deals, the agency issued separate checks to us and to the claimant and needed our entity tax ID number in addition to a copy of the claimant's driver's license and social security card.

Deed Review

You also want to view a copy of the deed that conveyed the property to the claimant. Who is listed as the owner on the deed? Is it the same person named as claimant? Is there more than one person named? Make sure all people named on the deed are on the claimant list or find out why they aren't. You need to make sure you have all the right people signing your documents.

You also want to copy the legal description of the property for your the limited power of attorney and it may be required for the claim form.

You can often view the deed online through the agency clerk's office or you can call and request a copy of the deed.

Agreement with Claimant

The second thing you need to do is get your agreement with the claimant signed ... NOW, while you and this claim are fresh on their brain and they are motivated to get it done.

Believe it or not, people will drag their feet even we you tell them they are owed thousands of dollars and you are going to help them get it. So let me make it very clear that you will be doing all the work and you have to take charge, tell the claimant what to do and when.

So first thing, get your contract for services signed immediately. We are paid on a contingency basis, if the claim is not paid, we don't get paid. So it is important to get your contract signed and start the claim process.

Sample Contract for Services

Disclaimer: This is just a sample power of attorney. You should seek legal advice regarding the format necessary in the area you are working in.

CONTRACT FOR SERVICES

By executing this Contract for Services, [PLEASE PRINT NAME] _____ ***Claimant*** of ***Claimant Address*,** ("Client"), agrees to the following provisions and hereby authorizes ***YOUR BIZ NAME*,** LLC, a ***STATE*** limited liability company, dba ***NAME ON LETTERHEAD*,** by its agents and representatives ("Company"), as Client's exclusive agent, to locate, prepare and process all documents, and receive and disburse all funds owed to Client directly, or indirectly as a trustee, authorized agent for a business entity, or as personal representative or heir of an estate, in the approximate amount of $ ***Claim Amount*** resulting from interest held in real property sold.

In consideration of preparing and processing claims for funds Company has located for Client's benefit and for the time and expense to locate Client, Client agrees that Company shall receive **40%** of the funds recovered. The Parties agree that Client will not pay any expenses and that Company's **fee is contingent on such funds being recovered.** Company is responsible for all expenses including research costs, document preparation, legal fees, filing and court costs associated with processing the claim and receiving and disbursing the funds. In the event that the funds are sent directly to Client instead of Company, Client is responsible for sending Company a check for its share of the funds within 2 days of receiving such funds. _____ Initials

Client agrees to sign and return all documents necessary to process the claim and receive the funds within 3 days of Company's request for such. Company will use all commercially reasonable efforts to obtain such funds. In the event that the claim is not paid, both Parties are released of their duties and obligations under this Contract for Services and Client will have no obligation to pay Company for any expenses it has incurred and shall hold Company harmless. This Contract for Services is binding on all heirs, successors in interest, and assigns.

This Contract for Services may be signed in counterparts and a signed copy received electronically or by fax shall be deemed an original. This Contract for Services shall be governed by the laws of the State of Texas. In the event a dispute arises, the venue shall be *AGENCY* Agency, *STATE*. The prevailing party shall be entitled to reasonable attorney's fees and other relief awarded by the Court.

In Witness Whereof, executed as of the date indicated below.

Date: _____   *NAME

ON LETTERHEAD*

_____   *YOUR

BIZ NAME*, LLC
Signature

_____   By:

Please Print Name   Title:

_____

Power of Attorney

You always need to get a limited power of attorney in every deal because this is what gives you legal authority to deal with the claim on the claimant's behalf.

The agency may require a copy or may require that the original be filed of record in the agency in order for them to recognize you as the claimant's agent, (sometimes called "attorney-in-fact" NOTE: not the same as attorney). The bank will also want to see the power of attorney if you are depositing checks into your account in the claimant's name.

Important Tips:

- Always get legal advice and check for legal requirements regarding a limited power of attorney in the region you are working in. Each state has different requirements regarding number of witnesses, specific language that must be included, whether it has to be filed in the agency to be legal, and agencies often have their own rules you have to follow as well. Some agencies require very specific language be included in the document and that you send them the original power of attorney.

- If you have more than one claimant, for example a husband and a wife both on the deed and both listed as claimants, you have to get each of them to sign his or her own power of attorney. They can not both sign one document; they each have to have their own.

- Always check with the agency recorders office to find out the filing requirements and filing fees. Most require a specific format; for example, that there are 3 inches of blank space at the top of the document so that their office has room on the document for its recording stamp and recording information.

- Always get your limited power of attorney notarized.

Assignment of Right to Claim

There may be a few instances when you are able to purchase the claimant's right to claim the excess funds. This is not a strategy you can use in every agency since many refuse to issue a check in the name of anyone other than the claimant. This is definitely a more advanced strategy and not recommended when you first start your business.

Working With a Notary

You will need the services of a notary public (also called "notary") for every deal you do. A notary public is defined as *"Someone legally empowered to witness signatures and certify a document's validity and to take depositions."*

Many of the documents you will be using in your business require a notary stamp. Since this is a virtual business you can do from anywhere, you will also need to services of a notary as a contact person to get your documents signed and returned to you quickly.

The notary can also do other tasks such as hand delivering the documents to the agency agency when "time is of the essence" and the claim must be filed immediately to get it in before the deadline.

Hiring a Notary:

It's pretty easy to find a mobile notary. Just do an internet search for "mobile notary" and the city and state. Here are a few sites you can use as well:

www.NotaryPublic.com
www.123Notary.com
www.GoMobileNotary.com
www.NotaryPhonebook.com

These sites are very easy to use and you can find all contact information for Notaries in all 50 states.

Contact several notaries in the area. You want to start a list of 3 or 4 you can call to handle deals for you in the area.

Important Considerations:

1. How much do they charge for their services?

Fees vary. Many notaries charge you by the number of signature pages. Some notaries add in extra charges for travel time as well. You have to be very specific as to where you want the documents to be signed. If the claimant is willing to go to the notary's office this is of course much less expensive for you. Generally, the notary will either be going to the claimant's house or the claimant's work location.

We have paid as little as $20 to as much as $50 to $60. I recommend calling at least 5 notaries to get price quotes. You will be surprised how greatly their prices can vary. We have called 5 notaries before and had prices ranging from $15 up to $95!

2.   What Is Included in the Service?

In addition to a notary certificate, your notary needs to have a cell phone and a digital camera. Agencies often require a copy of the claimant's drivers license as part of the claim process. The Notary will have to take a picture of their license and send that back to you. Make it standard policy to get a picture of the license every time.

3.   Payment Acceptance Options?

After you establish a price, you need to know in what forms the notary will accept payment. The easiest way is to pay is through PayPal after you receive all the documents. If you aren't familiar with PayPal it is a secure way to conduct transactions over the internet. It's fast, easy, and has zero hassles. I recommend this method first. Some notaries do not have PayPal accounts. If that is the case you will need to send them a check or money order instead.

4.   Agreement with your Notary:

You need to get a written agreement signed by your notary with clear instructions for how the signing order goes, where they will meet the claimant and at what time. Price and payment method will of course be included in this agreement as well.

5.   Claimant Meeting and Signing Order

Of all the steps in dealing with a Notary, this is by far the most important one. Your instructions to the Notary need to make it very clear that the documents are to be signed in a specific order, especially if the claimant has not previously signed your contract for services.

The Notary should do the following when meeting the claimant:

1. Either take a picture or get a copy of the claimant's drivers license and social security card for the notaries records and for the claim processing,

2. Get your Contract for Services signed first,

3. Get the Limited Power of Attorney signed and get witness signatures,

4. Get the W-9 signed,

5. Get the Claimant's Instruction Letter Regarding Check signed,

6. Get the Agency Claim Form signed,

7. Get any additional documents the agency needs signed,

8. Get claimant to sign notary book.

[**Important Tip:** You need this set of documents for EACH claimant. If you have husband and wife claimants, you will have 2 sets of each document.]

It is very important that the Notary follow this order. If your contract is not signed first, you may have a few claimants that try to get enough information to try to cut you out of the process after you have gone to the time and expense of finding them and informing them of the money.

The Notary will then overnight all original documents. If you mailed the documents to the notary, you can include a return FedEx label and envelope for easy return of the documents. We generally email the documents to the notary, have the notary print them and have the notary FedEx all the original documents back to us and bill it to our FedEx account.

Make sure you get a tracking number from the Notary so you know exactly where your paperwork is at all times. We will sometimes have the notary either fax or scan and email the documents to us prior to sending them overnight.

On a few deals, we were required to file the original power of attorney at the Agency recorder's office.

You can pay a notary extra money to handle this for you, or you can deal with the Agency yourself.

Action Items:

1. Start gathering the legal requirements for the area you are working in, i.e. What does the agency require? Do they have specific language they require in the Contract for Services, the Power of Attorney, or the claim form?
2. Start getting your general documents ready with your business information included. Then you can use a set of base documents and use the Find and Replace function in you word processor to insert claimant's name, address, etc. as you start each deal.
3. Get legal advice for any documents or laws you are unsure about.
4. As you do deals, keep contact information on notaries you like so that you have a quick reference of who to call for the next deal.

Section Six

Processing the Claim

Let's just run through the whole process start to finish. You got your list, did your skip tracing, and contacted the claimant. Claimant agrees to hire you. You want to line up your notary, get your documents signed and process your claim as quickly as possible.

1. If you haven't already, send an email to agency to find out exactly what documents are needed and get claim form,

2. Prepare Contract for Services and either email to claimant to sign and fax back the same day or include it in your packet you are sending to Notary for meeting with claimant,

3. Review the Deed to make sure you know who was on title at time foreclosure sale and to get copy of legal description of property sold at foreclosure

4. Prepare claim form and Claimant Instruction Letter Regarding Check for Claimant to sign,

5. Prepare Limited Power of Attorney, be sure to check for required number of witnesses or specific language required by that agency and for clerk's recording

requirements like specific margins for record stamping,

6.   Prepare a W-9 for claimant to sign (necessary to show that claims were released to claimant), you will want this even if the agency does not. Go to the Forms section at http://www.irs.gov to download a copy that you can fill in and print,

7.   Prepare your Notary Instructions regarding the meeting with claimant, the documents to be signed, and the order of signing,

8.   Prepare the Notary Agreement and email it to the notary to sign and fax back to you,

9.   Contact agency to verify once again that the claim exists and the list of all documents the agency needs to process the claim,

10.   Prepare the cover letter to the agency. Your cover letter serves as the "Summary" for what you are handing over to the Agency and why. Be sure it lists each document they request and be sure all those documents are included in your notary instructions and the packet of documents the claimant will sign.

You don't want to forget something and have to send the notary out to the claimant a second time.

It also needs to explain all of the relevant details of the transaction such as EXACT claim amount, year of foreclosure sale, claimant full name, parcel # and the most important part is……. Make sure you have the check to be sent to YOUR address NOT the claimants!!! We often include a pre-addressed pre-stamped return envelope addressed to:

Claimant's name

c/o my name
my address
city, state zip

11.   Email or mail your notary instructions and all the documents the claimant needs to sign to the notary. Schedule a time for notary and claimant to meet.

12.   Follow up with notary and claimant to make sure they have witnesses available for the signing.

13.   Have notary overnight all the original documents to you after the meeting with claimant.

14. Review all documents as soon as they come in and make sure all signatures and notary seal are present.

15. Send all the documents with your cover letter to agency. You need to give the Agency specific instructions for how to handle the funds, where to mail them to and how to contact you if they need to. Triple check the claimants required documents and notary requirements. FedEx all docs and track them. If they give you a PO Box mailing address, make them give you a non PO Box address. You cannot send FedEx packages to a PO Box!

16. Follow-up with agency to verify that they have received the documents and see if there is any additional information they need to process the claim.

17. If you have not heard from the agency, follow-up within the next 2 to 3 days.

18. Stay in contact with your claimant to let them know how the claim process is going.

Constant follow up is crucial with this. Using tracking numbers is definitely a top priority as well.

<u>Tip for Doing Follow Up With Agency:</u>

The easiest way to maintain follow up with Agency is through email. It is not always easy getting your agency contact on the phone. They are always busy helping other customers, so if you want to correspond by phone, be prepared to leave a lot of voicemails and play phone tag all day. I would suggest following up once every 2-3 days to check how the progress is going.

Dealing with the Bank/ Handling the Check:

Payday is what we are all waiting for and we are so thrilled when we get that check in after all our hard work. The bank is generally going to want to see your power of attorney if you are depositing a check into your account in the name of someone else so be sure you have the power of attorney to show them.

After you deposit the check, you generally wait a week or so to make sure there are no issues with the check or that the agency does not require anything further before you issue the check to the claimant for their share.

I can tell you from experience that even with all your best efforts and instruction letters, the agency will not always do things the way you ask and often will split the check or send the check to the claimant.

Preparing Thank You and Disbursement Letter

Draft a simple one page letter explaining the enclosed check amount for claimant's share of proceeds, thanking them for using your services and include a Testimonial Page and pre-addressed , stamped return envelope.

When mailing this, make sure to mail it CERTIFIED Return Receipt Requested so you have record that the claimant DID in fact receive their check.

Once the claimant gets his or her check, have them write up a testimonial for you. You should actually do this before you send the check if possible. Another option is to have a "testimonial clause" in your contract to ensure they give you a testimonial.

Section Seven

Fast Track Success Summary and Checklists

Don't worry about getting your system perfect, just get the list and make the contact. The more claimants you contact, the better you will get a closing the deal. This business just takes the right information, which you now have in this Success Guide, tenacity and perseverance.

Continually get your lists and keep all your contact information in your online data management system. When you find a claimant, focus on getting that deal done.

When dealing with the agencies, always remember that each agency is different. They all have different rules when it comes to how they run their departments. Always ask if they require special language in the claim form, power of attorney and what other documents they may require to process the claim. Pay attention to their margin requirements when recording a document. Pay close attention to their recording and filing fees, method of payments, contact person to send it to and correct mailing address for each department you deal with.

You have to really focus on the details with the paperwork in this business. If you aren't, it will cost you a lot of time and unnecessary expense. Get all of your required documents signed at once. The last thing you want to do is have to hire a notary twice for the same deal! One of our associates forgot to draft documents for the spouse, who was also on the deed, and we had to send the notary back out to the claimant to get the spouse to sign her set of documents. This meant extra notary fee and extra FedEx expenses that could have been avoided. Be sure your cover letter to the notary or the agency lists all the documents you need and then make sure all those documents are included.

When you are trying to find your Claimant, call every phone number on your skip trace report until you reach the claimant or someone who might know where claimant is located. Follow up with a letter or postcard to the claimant or the relative or friend you found with a good address.

Remember that you are the professional who processes these claims. Your confidence needs to come across in your phone calls and you need to back it up with your website and professional letterhead and marketing materials that further strengthens your credibility. Use lower dollar claims to practice your calls and your responses to common objections.

Dealing with notaries is usually very simple. The key is to spell out in your agreement EXACTLY what you need done and in what order and timeframe. One of the great things about working in the unclaimed funds business, is that you can live in New York and do deals in a agency in California. Use the notaries to do your leg work and the rest can be done by mail or email.

Remember the specific order of the paperwork signing too, this is very important and could cost you thousands of dollars if not done correctly. Remember not to give too much information before you get your contract signed.

Try to identify your problem areas and work to improve those. Devote some time to getting your system set up and then it is much easier and less stressful when you get those call-backs from the claimant.

My best advice is don't give up. You are going to make a lot of calls and some of the people are going to be down right rude, even when you are trying to help them put thousands of dollars in their bank account. Just remember that you are doing a great service for them because they would not have even know they have the opportunity to collect this money if you had not called them.

When you get a deal completed, pat yourself on the back. Think about it this way, retails stores have people walk in all day, if their lucky, but not all of the people are going to buy. Not all of the people you are going to call are doing to sign with you. It's just the way it is. So celebrate we you do get those deals and keep pushing forward. There are a lot of unclaimed funds out there and we're only focusing on one small area in that vast sea of unclaimed money.

Fast Track Checklists

The following are checklists for you to use to set up your business and for processing a claim. Use your checklist each time you do a deal so you don't miss an important step. This will help you stay organized and on top of the process. Good luck and Best Wishes on Your Success!

Business Setup Checklist

____ Decide on Business Name

____ See if you need Business License in your state; if so, get it

____ Register Domain Name for your website, go to GoDaddy here http://affiliate.godaddy.com/redirect/49 08F14899892BED6A119CFA31B0F43 82E930026E711546F827669EF6FD5 6B42

____ Create Website with Your Business Name & Logo

____ Rent Mailbox With Street Address if Not Using Home Address

http://www.theupsstore.com,
http://www.pakmail.com

____ Use E-mail Address Through Your Domain Name, not a gmail, hotmail or yahoo account

____ Decide if Sole Proprietor or Forming Business Entity, seek legal advice, file necessary paperwork

____ Apply for Tax ID Number if New Business Entity,
go to http://www.irs.gov to apply for an EIN

____ Get Toll Free 800 Number Service, go to Freedom Voice at
http://www.anrdoezrs.net/click-3765911-10683473

____ Create Business Cards and Letterheads with your Business Name and Logo

____ Set Up Bank Account

____ Join the Better Business Bureau

____ Sign Up with Skip-Tracing Company, go to one of following:
www.Accurint.com

www.Intelius.com ;
http://www.kqzyfj.com/click-3765911-10794544
www.MerlinData.com

___ Put Testimonials on your site – people want to hear about other people you have helped

Claimant Name
Filing Deadline: _____, 20__
Claimant Address
    Agency Agency, *State*

Claim Processing Checklist

___ Contact Agency:
    __ Confirm Claim Available;
    __ Get Claim Form,
    __ Get list of docs and special language required

___ Prepare Contract for Services: either email to claimant to sign and fax back
    or send to Notary for meeting with claimant,

___ Review the Deed: who was on title at time foreclosure sale; get copy of legal description of property sold at foreclosure

____ Contact Mobile Notary, verify has digital camera and understands instructions

____ Prepare Documents:

__ Claim Form,

____ Claimant Instruction Letter Regarding Check

____ Limited Power of Attorney, [check: (1) required number of witnesses or (2)specific language required by that agency and (3) for clerk's recording requirements like specific margins for record stamping,

____ IRS Form W-9

____ Assignment of Right to Claim [only if not doing a contract for services]

____ Mobile Notary Agreement

____ Mobile Notary Instruction Letter

____ Email or Fax Notary Agreement , have notary to sign and fax back to you,

____ Contact Agency to verify once again that the claim exists and the list of all documents the agency needs to process the claim,

____ Prepare Cover Letter to Agency, listing all the documents you are sending

____ Prepare pre-addressed pre-stamped return envelope to include with

letter to Agency, addressed to:
Claimant's name

c/o my name

my address

city, state zip

___   Contact Claimant : Schedule a time for notary and claimant to meet, verify that 2 witness will be available.

___   Email or mail docs to Notary, include:
__ Notary Instructions
__ Claim Form,
__ Claimant Instruction Letter Regarding Check
__ Limited Power of Attorney,
__ IRS Form W-9
__ Assignment of Right to Claim [only if not doing a contract for services]

___   Follow up with notary: confirm receipt of documents and instructions

___   Confirm docs overnighted and get Tracking Number from Notary.

___   Review all documents: make sure all signatures and notary seal are present

_____ Send all the documents with your cover letter to agency.

_____ Follow-up with agency to verify received the documents and see if there is any additional information they need

_____ If you have not heard from the agency, follow-up within the next 2 to 3 days.

_____ Contact Claimant to update on claim processing

_____ Receive check from Agency, make a copy and deposit in bank

_____ Call / Email Claimant and let them know you are sending check and ask that they complete the attached Testimonial and return it to you

_____ Send Funds to Claimant with Disbursement Letter and Testimonial Page

NOTES

Made in the USA
Las Vegas, NV
10 November 2023

80567463R00035